Jones Library, Inc.
43 Amity Street
Amherst, MA 01002
WITHDRAWN

Pebble Plus

Keeping Healthy

Taking Care of My Ears

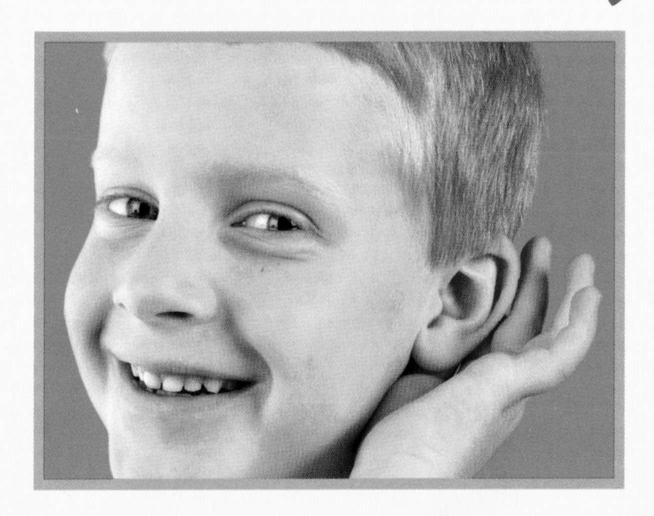

by Sarah L. Schuette

Consulting Editor: Gail Saunders-Smith, PhD

Consultant: Amy Grimm, MPH
Program Director, National Center for Health Education
New York, New York

Capstone press

Mankato, Minnesota

Pebble Plus is published by Capstone Press,
151 Good Counsel Drive, P.O. Box 669, Mankato, Minnesota 56002.
www.capstonepress.com

Printed in the United States of America

1 2 3 4 5 6 10 09 08 07 06 05

Library of Congress Cataloging-in-Publication Data
Schuette, Sarah L., 1976–
Taking care of my ears / by Sarah L. Schuette.
p. cm.—(Pebble plus. Keeping healthy)
Includes bibliographical references and index.
ISBN 0-7368-4259-4 (hardcover)
1. Ear—Care and hygiene—Juvenile literature. I. Title. II. Series.
RF136.S37 2006
612.8'5—dc22 2004026744

Summary: Simple text and photographs present information on how to keep your ears healthy.

Credits
Jennifer Bergstrom, designer; Stacy Foster, photo resource coordinator

Photo Credits
Capstone Press/Karon Dubke, all

The author dedicates this book to the memory of Palmer and Lena Schuette of Belle Plaine, Minnesota.

Note to Parents and Teachers

The Keeping Healthy set supports science standards related to physical health and life skills for personal health. This book describes and illustrates how to take care of your ears. The images support early readers in understanding the text. The repetition of words and phrases helps early readers learn new words. This book also introduces early readers to subject-specific vocabulary words, which are defined in the Glossary section. Early readers may need assistance to read some words and to use the Table of Contents, Glossary, Read More, Internet Sites, and Index sections of the book.

Table of Contents

My Amazing Ears 4
Checking My Ears 10
Healthy Ears 14

Glossary 22
Read More 23
Internet Sites 23
Index 24

My Amazing Ears

My ears help me
hear sounds.
Sound waves move
through the air.
My outer ears catch
the waves.

Sound waves go

into my ears.

The waves hit my eardrums.

My eardrums vibrate.

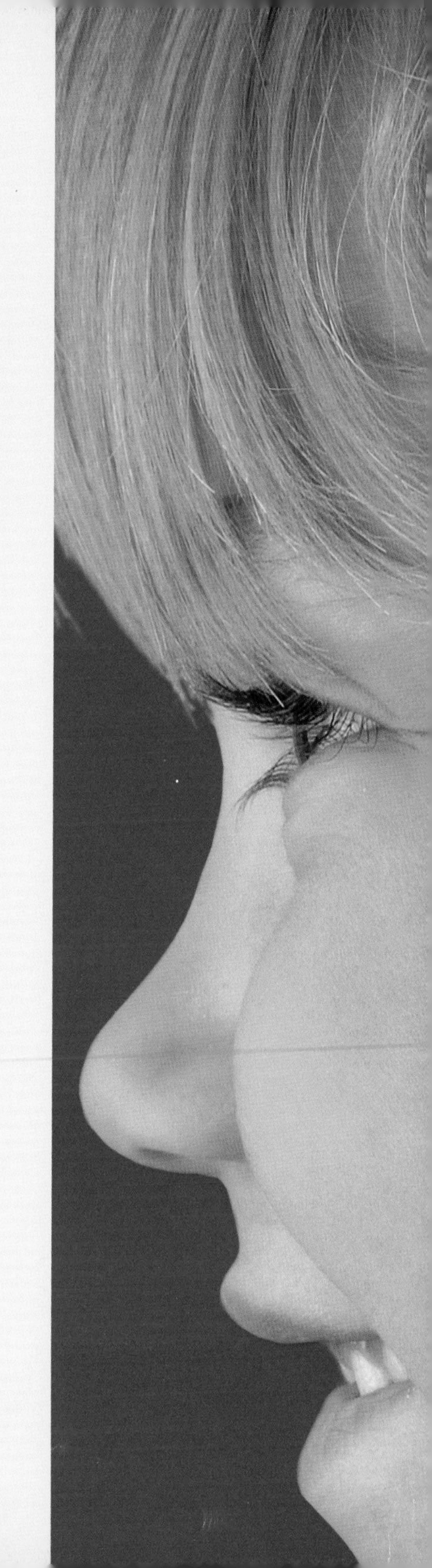

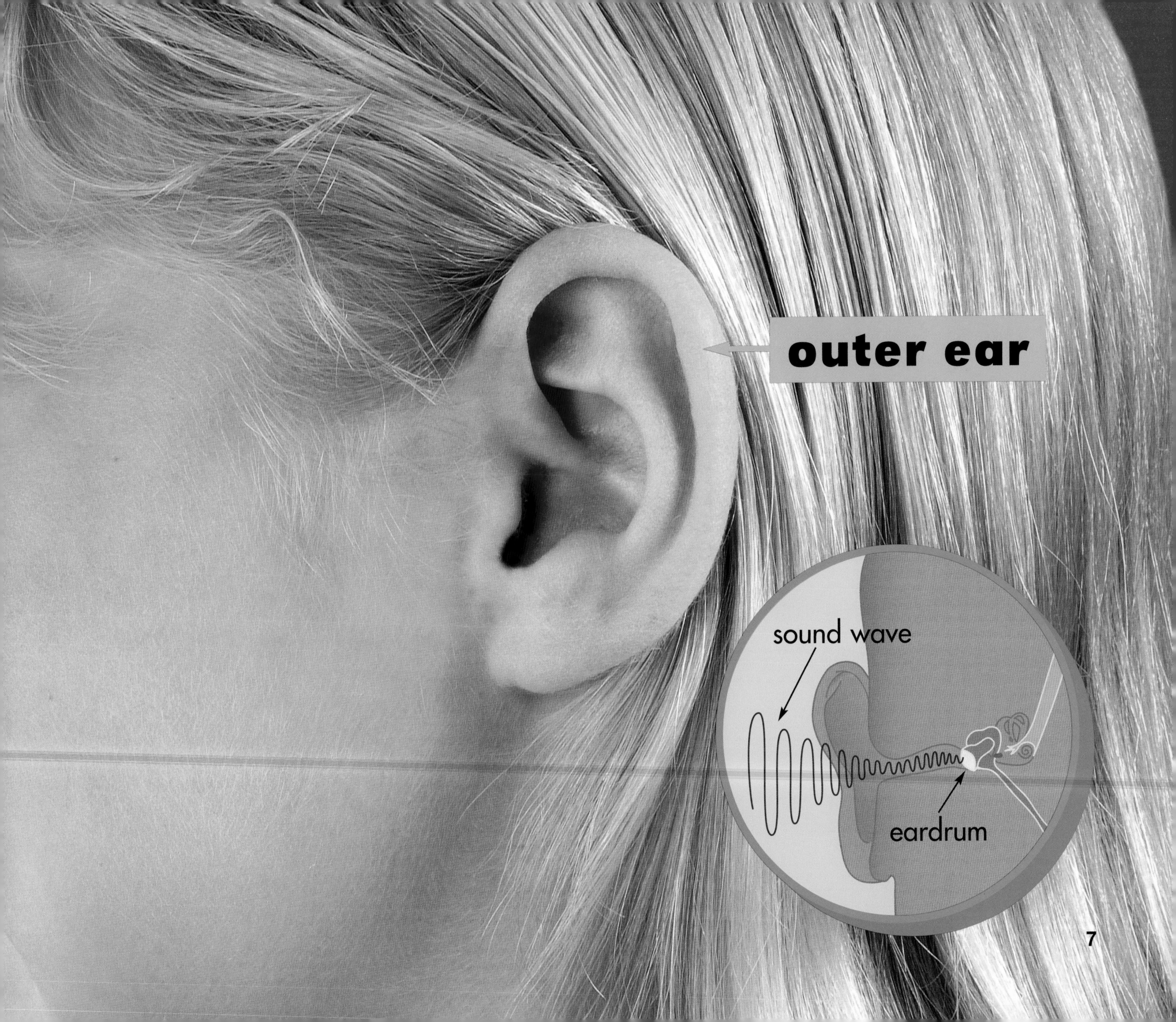
outer ear
sound wave
eardrum

The vibrations move
to my brain.
My brain understands
the messages.
Then I hear the sound.

Checking My Ears

I get my hearing
checked each year.
I wear earphones and listen
for high and low sounds.

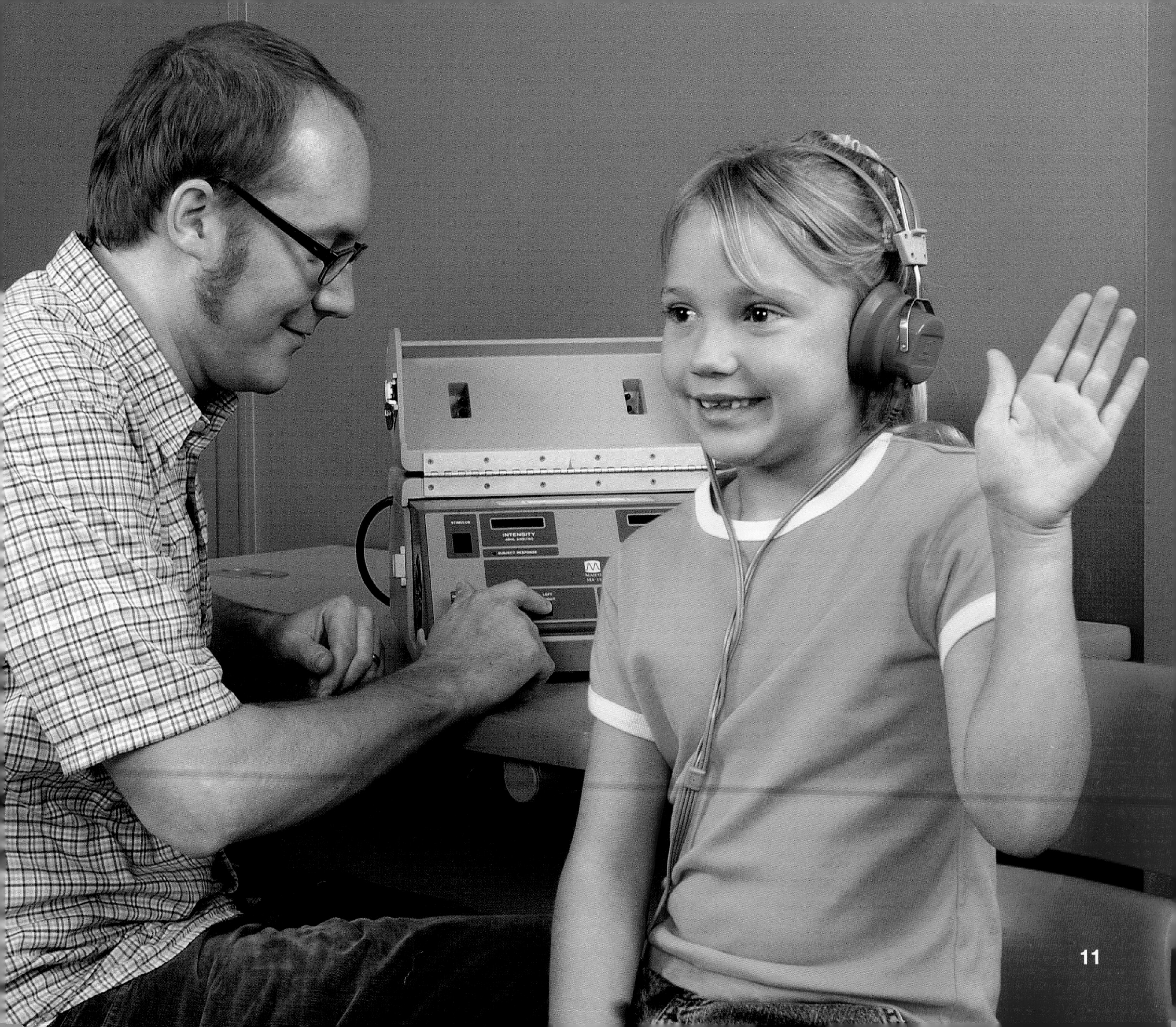
INTENSITY

I tell an adult when
my ears hurt.
A doctor checks
for an ear infection.
I take medicine
to feel better.

Healthy Ears

I keep my ears healthy.

I clean the wax

from the outside

of my ears.

I wear earplugs
when I go swimming.
I do not put anything else
inside my ears.

Loud noises can
hurt my ears.
I turn the volume down.

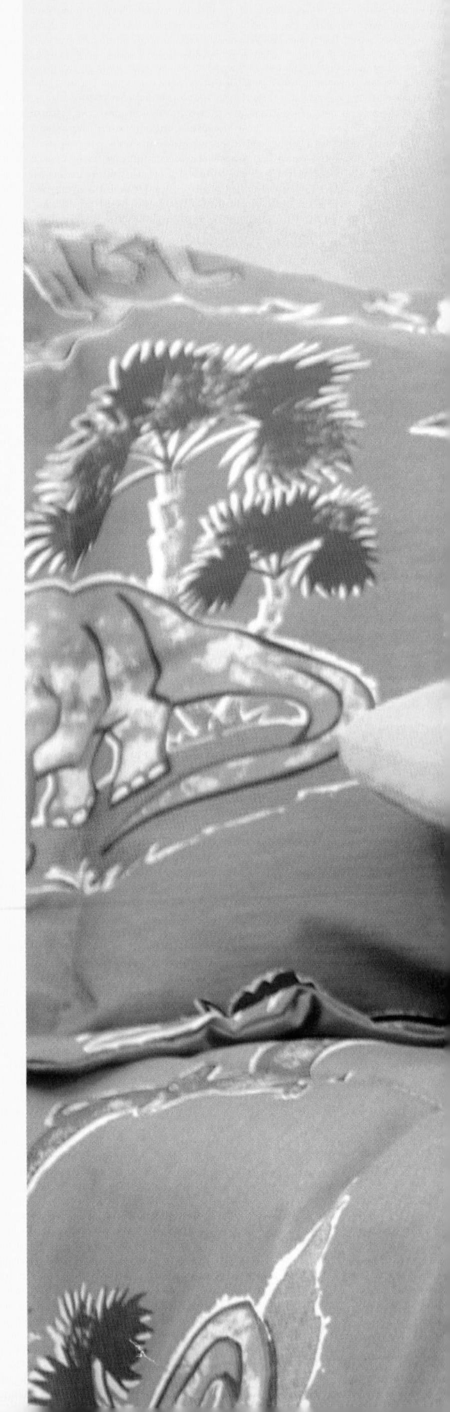

Taking care of my ears
helps them stay healthy.

Glossary

brain—the body part inside your head that controls your body; your brain understands what your ears hear.

eardrum—a thin skin inside your ear; the eardrum vibrates when sound waves hit it.

infection—a sickness caused by germs or viruses; infections can cause swelling and pain in the ear.

outer ear—the part of your ear that you can see

sound wave—a wave or vibration that can be heard

vibration—a fast movement back and forth

volume—the measure of how loud something is

Read More

Douglas, Lloyd G. *My Ears.* My Body. Danbury, Conn.: Children's Press, 2003.

Klingel, Cynthia Fitterer, and Robert B. Noyed. *Ears.* Let's Read About Our Bodies. Milwaukee: Weekly Reader Early Learning Library, 2002.

Rosinsky, Natalie M. *Sound: Loud, Soft, High, and Low.* Amazing Science. Minneapolis: Picture Window Books, 2003.

Internet Sites

FactHound offers a safe, fun way to find Internet sites related to this book. All of the sites on FactHound have been researched by our staff.

Here's how:

1. Visit *www.facthound.com*
2. Type in this special code **0736842594** for age-appropriate sites. Or enter a search word related to this book for a more general search.
3. Click on the **Fetch It** button.

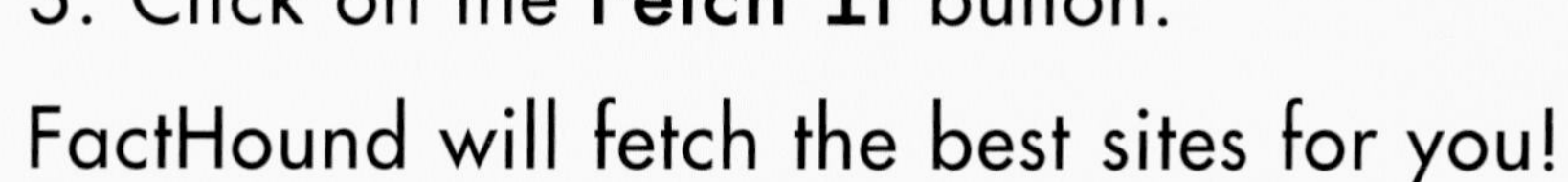

FactHound will fetch the best sites for you!

Index

brain, 8
clean, 14
doctor, 12
eardrums, 6
earphones, 10
earplugs, 16
infection, 12
loud noises, 18
medicine, 12
messages, 8
outer ears, 4
sounds, 4, 8, 10
sound waves, 4, 6
vibrations, 6, 8
volume, 18
wax, 14

Word Count: 137
Grade: 1
Early-Intervention Level: 16